Bipolar disorder

The complete guide to understanding bipolar disorder, managing it, bipolar disorder remedies, and much more!

Table Of Contents

Introduction 1

Chapter 1 Bipolar 101: Definition, Myths, Types, and the Thin Line that Separates it from Depression 2

Chapter 2 Causes, Symptoms, and Warning Signs to Watch Out For 9

Chapter 3 Diagnosis and Treatments for Bipolar Disorder 15

Chapter 4 Coping with the Disorder 21

Chapter 5 Helping Someone with Bipolar Disorder 23

Chapter 6 How to Distinguish Between Normal Mood Swings and Actual Bipolar Disorder 26

Chapter 7 How to Control your Manic & Depressive Episodes 30

Chapter 8 How to Educate/Tell your Family, Friends, and Colleagues About your Condition 34

Chapter 9 Natural & Holistic Approaches for Treating Bipolar Disorder 38

Chapter 10 New Research into Bipolar Disorder 42

Chapter 11 Is Bipolar for Life? 44

Conclusion 47

Introduction

I want to thank you and congratulate you for picking up the book, "Bipolar disorder".

This is the 2nd edition of this book, recently updated to make this a complete guide for anyone wanting to learn more about bipolar disorder. This book contains helpful information about what bipolar disorder is, and how you can manage it, and work towards overcoming it.

If you have bipolar disorder, this book provides all of the steps necessary to manage the condition. You will discover where to go for help, and what some of the key symptoms of different variations of bipolar disorder are.

If you have family or friends with bipolar disorder, this book will also serve as in informational guide that will help you better understand the condition.

You will soon learn how to deal with the condition, and what to do when a manic or depressive episode strikes. You will learn how to ask for help, and explain the condition to your friends and family.

This book will explain to you tips and techniques that will allow you to successfully manage your bipolar disorder and eventually improve it!

I hope this book will be able to help you better your understanding of bipolar disorder, and eventually manage and control it completely.

Thanks again for taking the time to read this book, I hope you enjoy it!

Chapter 1
Bipolar 101: Definition, Myths, Types, and the Thin Line that Separates it from Depression

So, what is bipolar disorder? This disorder is also popularly called manic depression (different to depression, but closely related). It can cause severe shifts in behavior, energy, mood, and judgment. It is more than just an ephemeral good or bad mood. Bipolar disorder cycles may last for a few days, weeks, or even months. The mood swings of people with bipolar disorder can be so intense that the said changes interfere with their ability to function well – the mood changes involved are different and more extreme than the usual mood swings that most people experience.

An individual with bipolar disorder might impetuously buy anything and charge the expensive amount to their credit card, quit from work, try a dangerous stunt, or may feel satisfied with a two-hour sleep during a manic episode. When there's a depressive episode, an individual might feel too tired to bring him or herself up after sleeping for eight hours. It's also possible that the person can feel hopeless and useless, particularly when stressful things occur such as having a huge debt that he or she needs to settle. Self-loathing may also occur as well as other negative feelings that can only make the situation worse.

The real culprit in the existence of bipolar disorder is still a mystery, but the condition often develops when someone else in the family has suffered from it or is currently coping with the disorder. The first depressive or manic episode normally occurs during the teenage years, or when the individual with bipolar disorder is still in his or her early adulthood. The symptoms are often subtle and somewhat confusing.

Due to the lack of information regarding the condition, the families and friends of people with bipolar disorder overlook the condition, considering a manic or depressive episode as a natural occurrence or a part of the sufferer's personality. The incorrect judgment or assumption of those around the patient may lead to greater suffering.

Unimaginable things can be prevented if proper support is given to those with bipolar disorder. Correct treatments can also help a lot in easing the symptoms, and together with the needed support and love, the bipolar victim will have a greater chance of experiencing a happy and fulfilling life.

The Truth Behind the Myth

There are several myths regarding bipolar disorder that only create more confusion in people's minds. There's a corresponding truth to every myth, which in turn can set things straight and bring an end to ignorance regarding the dreadful disorder. To help you in your quest to learn about the condition, here are some of those myths (as well as the corresponding truths):

Bipolar Myth 1: An Individual's Mood is the Only Thing that Gets Affected

Most people believe that the only thing that gets affected if a certain individual has bipolar disorder is the mood, but the truth is it affects the entire life of the sufferer. It affects one's memory, thinking, concentration, energy level, sleep patterns, judgment, sex drive, confidence, and even appetite.

Moreover, the disorder has also been linked to substance abuse, diabetes, migraine, heart disease, hypertension, and anxiety.

Bipolar Myth 2: The Sufferer will not be able to Recover or Live Normally

The truth is that there are people with bipolar disorder (some of them are famous celebrities) who have happy family lives, successful jobs, and almost-perfect relationships. These people experienced some difficulties at one point, but bipolar disorder did not stop them from living fulfilling lives.

Living with bipolar is not easy and, in fact, it can be very challenging, but it is not something that can stop anyone from having a normal life. Solid support from family and friends, together with the proper treatment, a healthy lifestyle, and good coping skills, can help the victim a lot. Anyone with the dreadful disorder can still live a normal and happy life while keeping the symptoms at bay.

Bipolar Myth 3: A Person who has Bipolar Only Lives with Alternating Episodes of Depression and Mania

The truth is that although there are times when a bipolar disorder sufferer may only seem to have alternating episodes of mania and depression. However, it does not mean that the sufferer will be like this for the rest of their life. Such occurrences do not last for long, especially if the patient gets correct treatment and receives support from both family and friends. There are times when mania or depression does not occur at all.

Sometimes, mania can be so subtle that it goes unnoticed. There are also cases where people with bipolar disorder can go for days or weeks without showing symptoms.

Bipolar Myth 3: Medications are the Only thing that can Keep Bipolar Disorder Symptoms Under Control

It is true that medications can help keep the symptoms at bay, but self-help strategies, therapy, support from loved ones, and having healthy habits (like following a well-balanced diet) also assist in keeping the symptoms of bipolar disorder under control. Doing worthwhile activities (such as working out and creating works of art) help the sufferer take his or her mind off the disorder. In other words, having fun is a good alternative to drugs.

It is also important to avoid stress. When the sufferer is feeling stressed, they can use simple strategies, such as getting a relaxing massage, listening to calming music, or immersing the body in a tub of warm water with some drops of aromatic oil. Aromatic scents can also help ease the mind and body.

All those myths regarding bipolar disorder are, at best, baseless. With the help of modern science, support, willpower, and belief that the disorder can be won, the condition will soon become a thing of the past.

Types of Bipolar Disorder

There are different types of bipolar disorder, and each type can be identified through their mania and depression episode patterns. The treatment that is best for an individual with the condition depends on the type of bipolar disorder that he or she suffers from. In order to give the appropriate treatment to that particular individual, a doctor must carefully examine and analyze symptoms to determine the type of bipolar disorder that's causing problems.

Bipolar I comes with mania and depression. It is considered the classic form of the disorder, and the most severe. What differentiates it from the other types? It induces at least a single manic or mixed episode. A large number (not all) of bipolar I sufferers have also experienced episodes of major depression.

Bipolar II involves hypomania and depression. A manic episode does not occur. Instead, bipolar II entails recurring episodes of hypomania (the gentler form of mania) and major depression. To be diagnosed with bipolar II disorder, the patient must have gone through at least one episode of major depression and one episode of hypomania. If a manic episode occurs, it only means that the patient has bipolar I disorder and not just bipolar II.

Cyclothymia is characterized by mild depression and hypomania. It is considered the mildest of all types of bipolar disorder. It involves cycles of mood swings. In spite of this, the alternating moods are not harsh enough to be considered major depression or mania. To be diagnosed with this type of bipolar disorder, the patient must have undergone several episodes of mild depression and hypomania within two years. To prevent cyclothymia from turning into a full-blown bipolar disorder, it should be closely monitored and treated accordingly.

Distinguishing Between Bipolar Disorder and Depression

Bipolar disorder is usually mistaken as depression because sufferers typically seek help when they are already in depressive stage. During manic episodes, patients fail to recognize that there is already a problem. Moreover, a number of people with bipolar are often more depressed than hypomanic or manic.

Know that the treatment for bipolar disorder is different from those for regular depression. The patient can end up in a risky situation if misdiagnosed. The antidepressant medication that is suitable for treating depression is potentially harmful to patients who have bipolar disorder. It is of utmost importance to choose a doctor who is well versed in treating the said disorder and knows how to recognize symptoms quickly.

Indicators that distinguish Bipolar Disorder from Depression

At a glance, bipolar disorder and depression can seem to be the same. It really is difficult to tell them apart. Luckily, there are indicators that can help solve the mystery and put an end to the dilemma. The following symptoms are the things to watch out for, as they're signs of bipolar disorder that aren't usually exhibited by those suffering from depression:

- Has gone through recurring episodes of major depression

- The initial episode of major depression happened before turning twenty-five years old

- When not in a depressive state, that person's energy and mood levels are usually higher than those of most individuals

- Someone in the family (or a first-degree relative) has had bipolar disorder

- The episodes of major depression usually last for less than three months (considered short)

- The sufferer usually loses his or her grip on reality every time an episode of depression occurs

- If the patient had experienced postpartum depression, then he or she is more likely to develop bipolar disorder later

Antidepressants are good for treating regular depression, but if the antidepressants stop working after being taken for months or if the patient has tried three or more kinds of antidepressants without any luck, then it is possible that the condition is actually bipolar disorder.

The treatments for bipolar disorder are different from those made for depression. In fact, the medications that are usually given to someone who is suffering from depression do not apply to patients with bipolar disorder. It is also foolish to self-medicate. Sufferers must consult a doctor as soon as possible to avoid developing further complications.

Chapter 2
Causes, Symptoms, and Warning Signs to Watch Out For

A person who'd like to know if he or she has bipolar disorder, should remain observant of the things that are happening to their body. Prevention is, and will always be, the best way to protect the body against the harmful things that try to attack it. Knowing the causes, symptoms, and warning signs of bipolar disorder can help prevent the dreaded disorder from becoming part of a person's life.

Causes and Possible Triggers of Bipolar Disorder

Bipolar disorder has many causes and triggers. Although there are cases where genes have something to do with the disorder, not everyone with a genetic history of bipolar disorder develops the condition. There are also cases where no one in the family had bipolar disorder and yet, one member still ends up suffering from it.

Certain medications, such as antidepressants can, set off an episode of mania. People who believe they have depression sometimes take antidepressants without consulting a doctor. Antidepressants can make bipolar disorder worse. Other drugs that can cause manic episodes are corticosteroids, appetite suppressants, medicines for cold (which can be bought over the counter), and medications for thyroid ailments.

Stressful events in life can cause bipolar disorder, especially to those individuals who are genetically susceptible to the said disorder. Stressful events usually involve drastic changes such as losing someone, getting married, losing a job, moving out, or going to college.

Sleep deprivation can also trigger a manic episode. Not having enough hours of rest can cause trouble to someone with bipolar disorder.

Substance abuse does not cause bipolar disorder, but it can trigger episodes and make things worse. Amphetamine, cocaine, and ecstasy are just some of the drugs that make episodes of mania much more likely to occur, while tranquilizers and alcohol can trigger episodes of depression.

Seasonal changes can trigger mania or depression. During summer, manic episodes are prevalent. Depressive episodes usually take place during spring, winter, and fall.

Signs and Symptoms of Bipolar Disorder

Different people with bipolar disorder don't usually exhibit the same signs and symptoms. There are patients who tend to have more manic episodes than depressive episodes, and vice versa. There are also others who only experience occasional occurrences of the different episodes.

Bipolar disorder actually has four types of mood episodes, namely mania, depression, hypomania, and mixed. Each of them comes with a unique set of symptoms. Of course, knowing these symptoms can help a lot in determining the type of episode that a patient is currently experiencing.

Mania Signs and Symptoms

During manic episodes, the patient may feel euphoric, highly creative, and extremely energetic. Patients who are experiencing episodes of mania often talk fast and practically don't stop. They are hyperactive and only need few hours of sleep.

Typical mania signs and symptoms are:

- Feeling unusually optimistic and ecstatic, or irritable to the extreme level
- Sleeping for only few hours, but surprisingly energetic
- Having unrealistic and ostentatious beliefs regarding his or her own capabilities or strength
- Speaking so rapidly that listeners find it hard to keep up
- Having so many thoughts at the same time
- Experience difficulty to decide or to judge, and is quite impulsive
- Staying focused is hard to do, and he or she gets easily distracted
- Acting without a care in the world, and not interested in the consequences of actions
- In severe cases, delusions or hallucinations

Mania may give a pleasant sensation at first, but it has a tendency to break out of control at any given moment. Most patients behave recklessly during an episode of mania. They engage in impulsive gambling, make foolish investments, seek sexual pleasure, pick fights, become angry, or blame others for their behavior.

Bipolar Depression Signs and Symptoms

Bipolar depression is different from regular depression. The two may seem to have close resemblance, but the treatments developed to fight them are different. Giving antidepressants (a known medication for depression) to a bipolar disorder sufferer will only make the situation worse. Nevertheless, it's crucial to watch out for these symptoms:

- A bipolar patient having a depressive episode tends to move or speak slowly (opposite of mania)
- There's a feeling of sadness, emptiness, and hopelessness
- The person may experience irritability, fatigue, or diminished energy, as well as fail to achieve any kind of satisfaction
- There are concentration, memory, and sleep problems
- Weight or appetite changes may likewise occur
- Some may experience mental and physical lethargy
- Suicide or death occupies the patient's mind

Bipolar patients may develop a condition in which they've utterly lost their connection with reality and fail to function properly at work and in social gatherings.

Hypomania Signs and Symptoms

Hypomania is also a mania, but in a less severe form. Patients experiencing episodes of hypomania may feel energetic, highly productive, and overjoyed. They can maintain their ability to perform tasks without losing their grip on reality.

Other people may view the episode as good mood, but at a higher level. The only trouble with hypomania is that the patient tends to make terrible decisions that may affect relationships, health status, and profession. There is always a possibility that hypomania may turn into a full-blown mania. Episodes of major depression may also follow it.

Mixed Episode Signs and Symptoms

A mixed episode triggers symptoms of hypomania or mania, together with symptoms of bipolar depression. Typical signs include racing thoughts, insomnia, irritability, anxiety, and loss of concentration. The combination of low mood and high levels of energy may result in a high risk of suicide.

Connection Between Bipolar Disorder and Suicide

The risk of committing suicide is prevalent among patients with bipolar disorder. That's why it is crucial to look after them all the time, because no one knows when an episode will take place.

A bipolar patient with suicidal tendencies may discuss death or suicide as if it's a natural occurrence and make it appear beneficial. The patient acts recklessly, as if orchestrating his or her own death.

There's a feeling of being helpless or hopeless, worthless, and useless. The patient may see him or herself as some kind of burden.

If there are signs that the patient is ready to commit suicide, it is best to act immediately and seek a professional who will be able to help him or her stay away from any act that could lead to death. A therapist or a counselor can usually extend the necessary help during such time.

Knowing the possible causes, signs, and symptoms to watch out for can help a lot in preventing bipolar disorder from creating an irreparable damage to the sufferer. It is best to seek immediate support and help, to avoid more complications.

Chapter 3
Diagnosis and Treatments for Bipolar Disorder

Bipolar disorder comes with its own diagnosis and treatment procedure that should not be interchanged with those for regular depression, even if the two conditions bear some similarities. Most medications being used in regular depression won't help someone with bipolar disorder, as they'll only make the problem much worse.

Diagnosis for Bipolar Disorder

Even professionals find it difficult to make an accurate diagnosis for bipolar disorder. Still, psychiatrists have the necessary experience to make a precise diagnosis and give appropriate treatment for someone who has bipolar disorder. Psychiatrists are doctors that specialize in mental health and keep themselves updated regarding the latest treatment options for such a disorder.

In order to diagnose bipolar disorder properly, an examination is carried out. It consists of a medical-history check, a physical evaluation, and a psychological assessment.

Currently, no lab tests can identify the presence of bipolar disorder. The doctor needs to analyze the medical history of the patient and conduct thorough physical examination to rule out illnesses with similar symptoms, or medications that might be responsible for the occurrence of the symptoms.

The doctor must be able to exclude thyroid disorder, adrenal disorders (such as Cushing's syndrome and Addison's disease), vitamin B12 deficiency, and neurological disorders (like multiple sclerosis and epilepsy), as well as medications for Parkinson's disease, antidepressants, anti-anxiety drugs, and corticosteroids.

During psychological evaluation, the doctor needs to know the complete psychiatric history of the patient. The doctor usually asks a series of questions about the symptoms, the time when the problem began to manifest, treatments or medications that the patient has received, and the family history in the context of mood disorders.

The doctor may also need to ask friends and family members about the behaviors and moods of the patient. Those people who are often around the patient can give a more accurate description of the patient's symptoms.

Treatment Options for Bipolar Disorder

There are different treatment options for individuals with bipolar disorder. After careful evaluation, the doctor will be able to give the correct treatment, which may include a combination of the available options. The treatment aims to relieve or keep symptoms at bay, restore the person's ability to function well, mend the damage that the disorder has caused, and reduce the chance of recurrence. Do understand that bipolar is a lifelong condition that can be tamed with help from correct medication, therapy, support from family and friends, healthy lifestyle, and the patient's willingness to win against the condition.

Taking mood-stabilizing medications can help a lot in keeping symptoms at bay, and in reducing episodes of mania and depression. It is almost impossible to prevent the condition from escalating into something more troublesome without the correct medication. However, taking the wrong medications can make the condition worse.

Therapy is also essential for people with bipolar disorder because they can learn how to cope with the disorder, especially when uncomfortable feelings emerge. It can also make relationships better, lead to better control of mood shifts, and even simplify stress management.

The lack of the needed information regarding the disorder can bring more frustrations on the part of the sufferer. Managing and preventing the symptoms should start by gaining thorough knowledge about the disorder. It is also best to educate friends and family regarding the disorder, to avoid misunderstandings that could sever good relationships.

Maintaining a healthy lifestyle can help a lot in keeping the episodes minimal in both frequency and severity. Keeping a regular schedule for sleeping, eating nutrient-packed meals, exercising regularly, avoiding triggers of stress, and getting enough sunlight everyday can improve a patient's condition.

The solid and continuous support of both family and friends can really help a lot in making the patient better, and that's why it is imperative for those people to get educated about bipolar disorder. Sometimes, the lack of needed knowledge or information about the illness can ruin a beautiful relationship, which can contribute to the worsening of the patient's condition.

Important Things to Keep in Mind when Taking Medication

Medication is essential for most people with bipolar disorder to help them keep their symptoms under control, or totally prevent those symptoms from emerging. It is important for the doctor and the patient to work well together to defeat bipolar disorder once and for all. There are cases in which a patient may need to try different medications under his or her doctor's supervision, to identify the one that will bring them the most benefits.

Patients should strictly follow the right schedule when it comes to visiting a doctor. Physicians, on the other hand, need to make sure that patients are still getting the correct dosages. In case the dosage needs to be changed, the doctor will give the specifics after doing some tests.

Medications are not miracle workers. Taking medication is not the only thing that a patient has to do in order to make everything all right. The medications can only reduce the symptoms of depression and mania. So, the patient should still try to follow a healthy lifestyle, get adequate rest, and take advantage of both the therapy and the support being extended.

The patient should continue taking his or her medication even if mood isn't a problem. Most individuals need to take their medications to avoid suffering from a relapse and to ensure that the disorder won't create any sudden trouble.

Therapy for Bipolar Disorder

According to research, patients who receive therapy, while taking medication, can manage their disorder better than those who do not get any therapy at all.

Bipolar disorder patients may find one of these three types of therapy beneficial:

- CBT or Cognitive Behavioral Therapy
- Family-focused therapy
- Interpersonal and social-rhythm therapy

In CBT, patients will learn how to examine thoughts that affect their emotions. They will also learn how to change negative thought patterns into positive ones. Bipolar disorder sufferers will be able to manage their symptoms and avoid triggers that may cause a relapse.

Family-focused therapy aims to eliminate the strain in marital and family relationships. It addresses the said issues and aims to restore a supportive and healthy home milieu. Educating the entire family about the disorder, learning the best ways of dealing with it, improving communication, and solving the problems at home without causing additional harm, are some of the things that the therapy intends to give.

Interpersonal and social-rhythm therapy concentrates on existing issues regarding relationships of the patient and improves the way a patient relates to the people that he or she cares about. By addressing and finding solutions to the said problems, this type of therapy can reduce the stress in the patient's life and may help reduce alternating mood cycles.

Social-rhythm therapy aims to stabilize the social rhythm of a person, which includes eating, sleeping, and exercising. When there's stability in the said rhythm, it is also possible for the biological rhythm that controls the mood to achieve stability.

Alternative Treatments

Most bipolar disorder alternative treatments are actually complementary in nature, and they aim to give better and faster results. Some of the alternative treatments that have proved to be beneficial are light and dark therapy, acupuncture, and mindfulness meditation.

Light and dark therapy bears some similarities with social-rhythm therapy, as both target the biological rhythm or clock of patients with bipolar disorder. Light and dark therapy aims to give an individual the correct light exposure, inducing proper sleep-wake cycles.

Currently, acupuncture is being considered as a complementary treatment to the disorder. Studies on acupuncture for regular depression have revealed that symptoms could be diminished significantly. Experts found increasing evidence that acupuncture might alleviate the symptoms of mania.

Mindfulness meditation includes breathing exercise and yoga, helping patients focus on the present situation and shatter negative thought patterns.

Keep in mind that the correct and proper treatment can only be given by the right specialist after making the necessary examination and evaluation.

Chapter 4
Coping with the Disorder

The most important thing regarding managing bipolar disorder is preventing a relapse from occurring. However, that's impossible to do sometimes. There are things that a patient can do when a manic or depressive episode occurs.

Things to do when an Episode Occurs

Don't focus on bipolar symptoms at a personal level; try to keep in mind that the symptoms are caused by an illness and not a byproduct of immaturity or selfishness. During an episode, an individual may do or say things beyond his or her control. Proper knowledge (about the disorder) on the part of the patient and those who around him or her can help a lot in understanding the situation and in preventing relationships from being damaged.

It is best to be prepared when destructive behaviors take place. While the patient is well, the sufferer and his or her family should talk about the things they need to do in case a destructive behavior suddenly occurs. Any misunderstanding will be prevented later on and panic will be lessened, if not eliminated.

It is best to have a crisis plan when something unimaginable occurs. Other than 911, it is best to have emergency numbers (such as numbers of the doctor, therapist, hospital, loved ones) handy by listing them and putting them up on a place where any family member can see the numbers. Include the address when possible. The numbers will come in handy, especially if the patient becomes suicidal.

What Family Members and the Patient Should Focus On

Living a healthy lifestyle (both the patient and the family members) can help a lot in managing the disorder. Giving the body the right amount of nutrients, having adequate sleep, getting a regular dose of exercise, staying away from unhealthy habits, and keeping stress to minimum can do wonders. Healthy living can keep anyone's focus away from harmful thoughts. It might even stop symptoms or episodes from appearing. Patients should take their medications regularly and make sure to follow the doctor's advice for any complementary treatment.

Seek support from each other. A bipolar patient does not always behave irrationally, especially if he or she is taking medications regularly. Bipolar disorder is an enemy that is quite difficult to deal with, but anyone can win against it with some help from the treatments that the doctor gives. As mentioned, emotional support and inner strength also lessen the condition's impact.

For the family, it is best to set boundaries and give only the amount of care that each member can extend, but make sure that everyone will be able to cover for someone else's shortcomings to avoid resentment. Do not let bipolar disorder take over your lives.

Chapter 5
Helping Someone with Bipolar Disorder

Bipolar disorder is not only difficult for the patient, but for other members of the family as well, including friends. The behaviors and moods of the sufferer can definitely affect all the people around him or her, even though these people want to help.

There are things that family and friends can do to help their loved one who's suffering from bipolar disorder.

Ways to Help

Bipolar disorder has the ability to drain the patience of people around the sufferer. Showing dismay or resentment may only make the sufferer feel worse.

It is best for family and friends to gain a deeper understanding of bipolar disorder so they recognize the things that are happening inside the head of the sufferer – all are beyond the ability of the sufferer to control. Learning about the disorder will make the family see that there are correct treatments for the disorder and there are things that they can do to keep the symptoms under control.

People surrounding the sufferer must have ample amounts of patience and stay understanding all the time. Those with bipolar disorder often refuse to see a doctor because they feel like they are introducing unnecessary burden to people around them. The family members and friends should be able to let the sufferer understand that they are there because they want to help, not because they feel obligated to show support.

Family members should be able to encourage the patient to seek medical help immediately to start the healing process. Delaying it will only make the healing process longer.

Never lose hope, though sometimes the case may look like a hopeless one. Encourage the patient more and hopefully, he or she will be able to feel that encouragement and begin to move on their own in finding ways to prevent bipolar disorder from ruining their life.

Supporting a Loved One

The best support that family or a friends can give to someone suffering bipolar disorder is to find a qualified doctor or therapist who can effectively deal with the disorder. Asking about doctors in the area who specialize in treating the disorder can help a lot.

During appointments, it is best to always accompany the patient. Tell the doctor the moods and behaviors of the patient to make evaluation easier and faster.

Learn everything about the medications and complementary treatments. Do not forget to track the progress. Close home monitoring can also prevent a possible relapse.

Call the doctor upon seeing any abnormal sign, or any development that can be considered unfavorable.

During an episode, it is best to spend some time with the patient (if not displaying aggressive behavior, otherwise call for help). If he or she has a surge of energy, invite the patient for a walk and have a great time together.

If the patient asks a question, be sure to answer honestly, but avoid confrontations or arguments (especially during an episode).

Never give out any personal comment because the sufferer may say or do things beyond his or her control.

Prepare healthy and easy-to-eat foods. It can be hard for the sufferer to sit down and eat his or her food properly during an episode of mania.

Make sure that the person gets adequate sleep at night and during a manic episode, let him or her take naps throughout the day.

If it is not easy for the family to take care of someone with bipolar disorder when episodes occur, imagine how difficult that experience is for the one with bipolar disorder. What people with such disorder need is love and support from their families, together with correct medications and complementary treatments.

Bipolar disorder can be defeated, but the sufferer needs the support and help of his or her family and friends.

Chapter 6
How to Distinguish Between Normal Mood Swings and Actual Bipolar Disorder

Everyone can be prone to mood swings from time to time. One moment they are in a very positive mood then the next moment they are in an extremely depressed state. Such swings can be triggered by external forces, but they can also be triggered by internal ones. It's not uncommon to see people who go from depressed to manic, and vice versa. However, that does not mean that this person has bipolar disorder. This is because there is a distinct difference between normal mood swings and actual bipolar disorder. This chapter will explain how to distinguish between the two.

To begin, one must define first what bipolar disorder is. Also known as manic depression, bipolar disorder is characterized by extreme mood swings that shift a person's mood from depression to mania and vice versa. Usually, extreme mood shifts occur only a few times within a year. For others, these swings occur as much as several times in a day or week. Generally, the severity of bipolar disorder is determined by how rapid the mood swings are and how extremely the behaviors are expressed.

While mood swings are generally considered as spontaneous events or products of an outburst of emotion, there is an underlying cause associated with bipolar disorder that causes a functional disruption at the level of the brain. While the exact cause is still unknown, there are a number of associated factors that may explain how such a disease develops. It can be of biological origin, as evidenced by physical changes in the brain. It can also be caused by imbalances in neurotransmitters that are naturally occurring chemicals that affect brain function. It can also be caused by genetic factors, as evidenced by the increased frequency of bipolar disorder among first-degree relatives.

According to the Diagnostic and Statistical Manual of Mental Disorders (DSM-IV), bipolar disorder is diagnosed by "the occurrence of one or more manic or mixed episodes accompanied by depressive episodes". If you'll follow such a description, any person dealing with depression who manifests at least 1 episode of mania could be diagnosed as having bipolar disorder. Such symptoms should not be the result of intoxication from substances such as alcohol or illicit drugs. Also, the symptoms should be severe enough that they compromise normal functioning, cause involuntary hospitalization, and/or cause harm or trouble to self and/or others.

To better understand how to properly diagnose bipolar disorder, one should know first the symptoms associated with both mania and depression (hence the alternate name manic depression). Here is how both conditions are defined:

Depression - Depression is reflected by a change in both mood and behavior. Mood alterations include a period of being sad, hopeless, worried or guilty. Also, depressed individuals may lose interest in things that used to be enjoyable for them. Behavioral changes include a general feeling of exhaustion, lack of concentration, restlessness, altered eating/sleeping habits, and suicidal thoughts. A depressed person may also show psychotic and catatonic features. A depressive episode may be defined by any of these symptoms/changes. A more conclusive diagnosis can be made if more of these are present in the patient at the same time.

Mania - Mania, just like depression, is also a state of altered mood and behavior. Mood changes observed in people during a manic episode include excessively aggressive behavior, extreme display of behavior, euphoria, agitation and paranoia. Behavioral changes include being unusually energetic, an increased propensity to talk, inflated self-esteem, and generally risky behaviors such as excessive spending, risk taking, and reckless actions. Manifestation of various forms of destructive behavior are also commonly observed in manic cases. Psychotic or catatonic symptoms may also be present during an episode.

Depending on how manic and depressive episodes manifest themselves, there are different ways to diagnose bipolar disorder. Here are 3 ways as to how a person with manic depressive symptoms may be diagnosed.

1. Bipolar 1 - This case is defined as the appearance of manic or mixed episodes that last for at least 7 days and/or severe enough that the person needs to be hospitalized. Such episodes almost always come with a preceding depressive episode. The usual behavioral pattern observed in Bipolar 1 patients show depressive episodes alternating with manic episodes. However, for bipolar 1, the presence of depression is not a prerequisite for diagnosing a patient.

2. Bipolar 2 - This case is similar to Bipolar 1, but there are 2 critical differences. First, Bipolar 2 involves episodes of hypomania, and second, the presence of at least 1 depressive episode is required. In contrast with Bipolar 1, Bipolar 2 patients do not present full-blown manic or mixed episodes. Noting this, the usual behavioral pattern observed in Bipolar 2 patients is

depressive episodes alternating with hypomanic episodes.

3. Cyclothymia - While this is not considered as a full bipolar disorder, people with cyclothymia show shifting episodes of mood changes similar to bipolar. The only difference is that the symptoms are milder.

While mood swings are generally spur-of-the-moment events and are generally self-limiting, bipolar disorder follows a pattern, has an underlying cause, and is generally persistent. If left untreated, this disorder can have a serious effect on the patient's life. At the same time, other people surrounding him/her can also be adversely affected. Episodes linked to bipolar disorder lead to disruptive behavior that can wreak havoc in both personal and professional ventures. Sufferers are also more prone to substance abuse. At its absolute worst, because of its links to suicide, it can cost the life of the patient and even those surrounding them.

As you can see, there are quite large differenced between bipolar disorder and regular mood swings. Changes in mood are a natural part of life that everyone experiences. On the other hand, bipolar mood swings are much more intense and dangerous.

Chapter 7
How to Control your Manic & Depressive Episodes

Bipolar disorder and other associated conditions can be very difficult to deal with because of their generally unpredictable nature. The best approach to keep this disease from overwhelming you and ensuring you have better control of your life is to manage both manic and depressive episodes that may arise during an attack. This chapter is a collection of practical tips on how you can control both manic and depressive episodes.

1. Dealing with Depressive Episodes

Dealing with depression can be taxing in so many ways. It has the power to eliminate a person's energy and will, making it difficult for them to live their life or just feel okay with being themselves. While dealing with depression is difficult, it is certainly not impossible. Learning to control and manage your depression will take some time, but it's 100% something that you can do!

The first step in dealing with depressive episodes is to take things one step at a time. You can't expect yourself to banish the effects of depression right away, but each small step will help. Some of the things you'll have to do to control depressive symptoms are difficult but you have to keep in mind that such actions are essential. Start with a few small goals and work your way up one day at a time. All those seemingly small steps will eventually take you where you want to be.

The second step in dealing with depressive episodes is to make an effort to build better relationships. You can get to know new people and build on the relationships you already have at the moment. One of the best ways to combat depression is to surround yourself with people who care, who will make you feel loved, who will give perspective when you need it the most. For some people, reaching out may seem overwhelming. However, you should never be afraid or guilty about doing it. Reaching out doesn't mean you'll be a burden to others. It simply means that you recognize the value of having them around.

The third step in dealing with depressive episodes is to eliminate negative thoughts. One of the most pervasive things about depression is dealing with negativity. When you're depressed, there seems to be a dark cloud hanging over everything. Getting negativity out of your system takes more than just "thinking positive". It's a multi-step process to achieving balance in your thoughts. You've got to stop being too hard on yourself. You got to stop aspiring for perfection but instead aspire to be at your best. You got to find the things that trigger your negative thoughts and consider if such thoughts are warranted. A great place to start is by using positive affirmations daily.

The fourth step in dealing with depressive episodes is to take care of yourself. One of the reasons people stay depressed is because they let themselves go. You've got to learn how to manage stress and adopt healthy habits. As much as possible, get sufficient sleep as it helps in reducing stress and fatigue levels. You also need to get enough exercise and get exposed to a little sunlight every day. You can also practice different relaxation techniques. Try yoga, meditation, or even a quiet walk through nature each day.

2. Dealing with Manic Episodes

Mania can be very difficult to control because it usually takes you to the edge of your limits. While it can be highly invigorating at times, manic episodes can decrease your productivity, cause you to take unnecessary risks and actions, and can even put your life at risk. While it can be difficult to deal with manic episodes at times, they can actually be managed using particular techniques. Furthermore, there are situations when you can even use your condition to your advantage! Here are some of the best ways to deal with manic episodes.

The first step in dealing with manic episodes is to have a plan before an attack even ensues. This will give you a better chance to deal with the effects, should they start emerging out of the blue. You can use the help of other people around you as they can serve as your monitors. You can ask them for feedback about your behavior. Based on what they say, you can create a plan of action for how you can better manage that specific situation, should it arise once again in the near future.

The second step in dealing with manic episodes is to take the side of caution. You have to find ways to reduce the risk of harm in the effect that a manic episode occurs. For example, if you have a predisposition for gambling or overspending, it would be wise to manage your daily budget, carrying only as much money as you need to survive the day. Also, if you have a propensity for abusing substances, make sure to stay away from such substances and the places where you can get them. Such an approach will at least minimize the potential of you doing something you'll regret later.

The third step in dealing with manic episodes is to make use of your extra energy in a positive way. It is a fact that bipolar people are among the most creative ones out there, as long as they are in a system where they can channel their energy properly. You can get into a fitness program, try out arts (e.g. painting, music), or learn a new skill. Such an approach will not just help you be more productive, but it will also allow you to gain more confidence!

Chapter 8
How to Educate/Tell your Family, Friends, and Colleagues About your Condition

One of the most difficult things about living with a mental disorder such as Bipolar Disorder is the fact that you have to explain it to other people, especially those who don't really understand what your condition is all about. What's more, you cannot expect that all the people you meet, even those you live with on a daily basis, will understand that you have a medical condition that's messing up your behavior. In spite of this, letting the people around you know about your condition is the best way to get much-needed support. This chapter will serve as a guide for educating and talking to your friends, family and colleagues about your condition.

1. You don't have to keep it as a secret

Partly due to the stigma associated with any form of mental illness, a lot of people who get diagnosed with bipolar disorder choose to keep it as a secret. Not only does such an action prevent others from understanding your predicament, but keeping such a big secret from others can also eat at you from the inside.

Understand that you don't have to keep your condition a secret. In fact, the best way to deal with a mental illness such as bipolar disorder is to just come out in the open about it. It will take a lot of courage to do so because you leave yourself open to prejudice, but think of it as something you have to do, not only for your own peace of mind, but also because your friends, family and colleagues deserve to know because they care for you.

2. You have to know that not everyone understands your predicament

It's a fact that even though there are a lot of efforts that aim to increase awareness of this disorder, most people still don't know or understand what bipolar disorder is all about. Oftentimes, it is either they completely have no idea about this condition or they have an incorrect understanding of it. Regardless, you need to understand that not everyone knows or understands your disease and how you're dealing with it on a day-to-day basis. Instead of getting discouraged when they don't understand you, take it as a challenge to educate them even further. More often than not, it's from you where they will have their first (and best) exposure on what bipolar disorder is. Maybe you'd like to lend them this book!

3. Talk about the basics of Bipolar Disorder

The best way to begin educating others about any kind of disease or disorder is to tell them the basics. To begin opening up about your condition, start with talking about what bipolar disorder is. You have to communicate to others that bipolar disorder is a legitimate disease that affects how your brain functions. Explain to them that this disease has existed for thousands of years and that doesn't necessarily mean that you are mentally incompetent or retarded. You don't have to be all technical about your explanation unless they insist to listen. Oftentimes, this knowledge is more than enough to instill in them what you are dealing with and why you need their support.

4. Talk about the symptoms of Bipolar Disorder

After mentioning that you have bipolar disorder, the next step is to explain to them the associated symptoms. This will give other people a heightened awareness about the signs that you will usually manifest, especially when you have an attack. Aside from explaining the symptoms themselves, you can also explain any scientific or technical terms associated with these symptoms. While there are many approaches to do this, one of the best ways is to explain it using layman's terms. Also, it will help to keep explanations simple. Among the most important things that you should explain, especially to people who you are with most of the time, are the potential life-threatening symptoms you may manifest, so they'll know what to do in the event that you get in trouble.

5. Tell them the harsh realities of the disorder and its effects

There are a number of realities you have to deal with as a patient of bipolar disorder. Sharing these realities is also considered as a must so that your family, friends and colleagues will better understand what you are going through. This may be quite difficult, as it will force you to open up about the hardships you experience when you're having a manic or depressive episode. You can tell them what happens to you and what you feel when you are depressed or in a state of mania or hypomania. Though it may prove to be taxing for some, being as honest as possible is highly helpful. If you don't feel comfortable about opening up about this stuff yet, you can start with the people who understand you the best, that you are the closest with.

6. Have the patience to educate and explain

Education is something that doesn't happen overnight. You can't expect others to understand your predicament immediately. There will be times when you have to explain to people about your condition over and over again. Take time to answer their questions, as there's a huge chance that you're the only place they will learn about bipolar disorder. Last but not least, never brush questions off as this could potentially make stereotypes about your condition worse. Having people around you understand what you're going through will help them to better support you and make managing your condition much easier.

7. Have a positive outlook about your condition

Aside from being a beacon of awareness about bipolar disorder, as a patient, you can also be a beacon of hope. The last thing you want is to overwhelm people around you and make them start thinking that this condition should feel like the end of the world. You have to tell them that bipolar disorder is a treatable condition and should it be successful, you are more than capable of living a normal and productive life. Through your actions and by having a positive outlook, you'll show others that there is hope if you have bipolar disorder.

Chapter 9
Natural & Holistic Approaches for Treating Bipolar Disorder

Bipolar Disorder is a mental illness with a complicated onset and far-reaching effects on how the human brain functions. Today, people are armed with better knowledge about this condition, and you can now find many different forms of treatment available. While going for pharmacological treatments is effective for treating both bipolar disorder and its symptoms, there are limitations to their effectiveness. Furthermore, there is also the potential that such treatments may cause other effects that may pose a threat to the person's overall health.

Because of the clear and present danger of relying on pharmacologic treatments, people are looking for other alternative treatments that are equally effective but less dangerous. It has been shown in studies that a more holistic approach in treatment provides better health outcomes for bipolar patients. This is because there are many contributing factors that cause this disease and trigger its symptoms. One of the biggest advantages such approaches provide is that most of them can be done from the comfort of your home, without causing any disruption to your daily life. Given these facts, this chapter will focus on the various natural and holistic approaches for treating bipolar disorder.

1. **Healthy lifestyle -** Based on the biopsychosocial model of medicine, ailments of the body can cause ailments of the mind, and vice versa. Taking this into consideration, leading a healthy lifestyle can have a positive effect on people with bipolar disorder. For example, regular exercise can help in steadying your

mood as it fights stress. It also causes the release of hormones such as endorphins, which help in making you feel happy and relaxed. Getting enough rest and sleep will also help in managing your symptoms as exhaustion and lack of sleep put excessive stress on the person and can also trigger mood swings.

2. **Balanced diet** - Following a balanced diet can also help in treating bipolar disorder in different ways. Getting proper nutrition through food is crucial in ensuring that your body runs at optimum levels. While there is no specific diet recommended for treating bipolar disorder, there are specific benefits you can experience from proper eating habits. First, it can help you to reach an ideal body weight. It has been shown in studies that those with bipolar disorder are more prone to becoming overweight. Second, sufficient nutrition has been proven to have a protective effect against this condition and many other diseases.

3. **Health supplements** - Taking nutritional supplements can help in improving overall health and managing specific symptoms associated with bipolar disorder. Omega-3 fatty acids seem to help improve the depression associated with bipolar disorder. While further studies are still being done to prove this, it has been observed that people with sufficient omega-3 consumption are less prone to depression.

St. John's wort is a supplement that has always been associated with treating depression. Other studies show that the supplementation of magnesium helps in lessening mania and the cycling of bipolar symptoms. While further investigation regarding the use of health supplements is underway, they are seen to have potential as supportive treatment for bipolar symptoms.

4. **Stress management** - Managing stress is one of the most important things to do if you are dealing with any kind of mental disorder. This is because stress may induce mood swings and other adverse effects associated with bipolar disorder. There are many ways to deal with stress. First, you've got to lessen the burden you place on yourself. Second, you have to strive to have a positive outlook. This can be developed through regular goal setting, and the use of affirmations. Third, you have to be in the right relationships and eliminate unhealthy ones. How you cope with stress has a huge impact on how effectively you can manage bipolar disorder.

5. **Alternative medicine** - This is a group of interventions that remain largely untapped for treating bipolar disorder. However, their historic effectiveness for treating numerous human ailments makes them potentially intriguing approaches for managing this mental illness. Tai chi, meditation and yoga are traditional practices that help in relaxing the mind and body, which is a must for keeping manic and depressive symptoms at bay. Acupuncture is also a safe and potentially effective treatment for depression and other bodily ailments.

6. **Psychiatric therapy** – Seeking the help of a psychiatrist is your best hope in managing bipolar disorder on a long-term basis. A psychiatrist is a doctor who is trained to treat mental illness. They can also help in either ruling in or out bipolar disorder and other forms of mental disease. The kind of approach the

psychiatrist and their team will use depends on the individual's current health state. Support and counseling will help you get to know your condition better and avoid situations that can potentially trigger symptoms. They can also assist you in living a normal life in spite of having bipolar disorder. They may recommend drugs or refer you to a treatment facility if the severity of your condition deems it to be necessary.

Chapter 10
New Research into Bipolar Disorder

Bipolar disorder is one of the most important psychiatric conditions out there. Because of its far-reaching effects and the relatively high number of people affected by it (aware or otherwise), it is considered as one disease that deserves higher attention from the medical and scientific community. This condition continues to be a good subject for research, with each discovery helping in better understanding this still highly misunderstood condition. Here are some new research studies into bipolar disorder.

The American Heart Association has recently announced that teenagers with bipolar and major depression disorder are at a higher risk of having heart disease and should be both considered as independent risk factors. Previous studies have uncovered that mood disorders have an association with increased risk of heart disease in adults. Other studies specifically mentioned major depression and bipolar disorder as factors that increase the likelihood of developing heart disease at an earlier age. On this note, early action to treat mood disorders is seen to lower the risk of heart disease.

Researchers speculate that there's a possibility that genetic links exist between creativity and psychiatric illness. A research team led by Robert Power of King's College in London published these findings in the journal Nature Neuroscience. Analyzing data from 86292 people from Iceland obtained from the biopharmaceutical company deCODE Genetics, Power and his team found that those who have creative professions are 25% more likely to carry gene variants related to bipolar or schizophrenia compared to the general population. Such findings suggest that these people may have a genetic pre-disposition towards "thinking differently"

A new study recently presented at the 28th European College of Neuropsychopharmacology Congress in Amsterdam, Netherlands has uncovered that adverse behavioral patterns such as risky behavior, impulsivity and psychomotor agitation occur in up to 50% of all suicide attempts. Analyzing 2811 patients with depression, parameters such as family history, previous suicide attempts, psychiatric symptoms, and the presence of disorders such as bipolar disorder, patients who suffer from mixed depression (as observed in related psychiatric disorders such as bipolar and cyclothymia) are at a higher risk of committing suicide. A recommendation was made that assessing such symptoms in depressed patients has "immense therapeutic implications".

A research published in the October 28, 2015 issue of the journal 'Nature' has proposed that brain cells of patients with bipolar disorder are more sensitive to stimuli in comparison to normal brain cells. Such a study is important as it shows at a cellular level how such a condition affects the brain.

Chapter 11
Is Bipolar for Life?

Given the potentially huge impact on a person's life and those around them, it's no surprise that a lot of people are worried about having bipolar disorder. Once they have it, is there any escape available? Sad to say, there is no escaping the effects of bipolar disorder as there is no cure available yet. Future research may hold the key to the discovery of better treatments and prevention techniques. However, through behavioral therapy, self-management and the use of medications, even people with bipolar disorder have the power to live a normal life. In fact, there are people throughout history who experienced success in spite of being bipolar. Here are some examples of successful people with bipolar disorder, proving that this disorder need not be your downfall.

Jim Carrey

James Eugene Carrey, more popularly known as Jim Carrey, is an actor, comedian, screenwriter, film producer and impressionist. He is known for his very energetic performances and is currently one of the biggest Hollywood stars. However, despite his success in his career, he has battled depressive episodes. He took medications, but eventually stopped. He has since said that he does not take stimulants, including coffee or medications anymore.

Carrie Fisher

She is an actress, performance artist, novelist and screenwriter. If you are a fan of Star Wars, you would probably recognize her as the actress who portrayed Princess Leia Organa. She is also known for Postcards from the Edge, a semi-autobiographical novel. Despite her success, Fisher has struggled with bipolar disorder, cocaine addiction and an addiction to prescription medication.

Henry Graham Greene

He was an author and novelist, and is actually among the greatest writers of the 20th century. Due to his popularity and literary acclaim, he built a reputation as a great writer, both for thrillers and serious Catholic novels. However, despite his popularity and success, he also battled bipolar disorder.

Ernest Hemingway

He was a short story writer, journalist and novelist. His understated and economical style made him strongly influential to fiction during the 20th century. In 1954, he was awarded with the Nobel Prize in Literature. Most of his works are regarded as American literature classics. He also had bipolar disorder.

Catherine Zeta-Jones

She is a popular actress who has received numerous accolades and critical acclaim throughout her career. She has won Screen Actor Guild Awards, an Academy Award, and a BAFTA Award. She also became the Commander of the Order of the British Empire as well as named Hasty Pudding Woman of the Year by the Hasty Pudding Theatrical society. However, despite all her fame and success, she suffered from bipolar II disorder.

Chris Brown

He is an actor, dancer and recording artist. He is actually one of the most popular R&B artists today. Ever since his self-titled debut studio album in the early 2000's, he has garnered fame and success. His album, Exclusive, went double platinum. Chris also suffers from bipolar disorder.

Jesse Jackson, Jr.

He is a former Democratic American Congressman and the son of Jesse Jackson, a former presidential candidate and activist. He represented the second congressional district of Illinois from 1995 until 2012. Aside from having a consistent liberal record on fiscal and social issues, he also co-authored books on personal finance and civil rights. However, on November of 2012, he resigned from Congress, citing physical and mental health problems, such as gastrointestinal problems and bipolar disorder.

There are plenty of other celebrities, models, political figures, authors, filmmakers, artists, socialites, and other high profiled individuals who are successful with their careers, even if they are suffering from bipolar disorder. This proves that bipolar disorder is treatable and controllable. So if you have this disorder and you still want to live a normal life, you should seek treatment as soon as possible and do your best to manage it.

Conclusion

Thank you again for downloading this book!

I hope this book was able to help you learn more about bipolar disorder.

If you personally suffer from bipolar disorder, don't lose hope. Follow the strategies in this book and begin working towards improving your condition!

If you have a family member or friend with the condition, I thank you for taking the time to read this book. I hope it has helped you better understand the condition.

The next step is to put the information you've found here to good use, and begin implementing some of the strategies that can help you manage your condition, or the condition of your loved one.

Finally, if you enjoyed this book, please take the time to share your thoughts and post a review on Amazon. It'd be greatly appreciated!

Thank you and good luck!

Check Out My Other Books Here:

Simply follow the links below to have a look at the other great books that I have available on Amazon! I specialize in mental health and self-esteem/confidence, and am sure that one or more of the following will be able to help you:

- Overcoming PTSD: http://amzn.to/1rx5X6E
- Social Anxiety Cure: http://amzn.to/1ytqm1a

- Mood Swings Solution: http://amzn.to/1ut0ZK9
- Understanding Schizophrenia: http://amzn.to/1svVevi
- The Anxiety Cure: http://amzn.to/1roPJvR
- The Self-Esteem Workbook: http://amzn.to/1u2Cr9i
- Overcoming Depression: http://amzn.to/1ytqygG
- Panic Attacks Cure: http://amzn.to/1mwxHHJ

www.ingramcontent.com/pod-product-compliance
Lightning Source LLC
LaVergne TN
LVHW021740060526
838200LV00052B/3383